E COMMERCE

:: Author ::

KINCHIT PARESHBHAI SHAH

(M.COM., C.A. – CPT., P.G.D.T.P(Gold Medalist)., SLET)

PUBLISHED BY

Chakravarti Sidhdhharaj Jaysinh International Publishing House

HQ. At & Po. Chaveli., Ta- Chansma,
Dist- Patan, North Gujarat, India, Asia.
www.iphouseindia.com

E COMMERCE

First Publication: 19TH FEBRUARY, 2015

Copyright: Author
(c) KINCHIT PARESHBHAI SHAH

ISBN:- 978-15-08712-52-7

Price: Rs.750/- INDIA
          $ 15 OUTSIDE INDIA

PUBLISHED BY

Chakravarti Sidhdhharaj Jaysinh International Publishing House
HQ. At & Po. Chaveli., Ta- Chansma,
Dist- Patan, North Gujarat, India, Asia.
www.iphouseindia.com

Dedicated to my Parents

Introduction to E Commerce and Internet

We are living in the age of technological advances. Development in our society began to happen post the World Wars, where in Industrial revolution started changing the face of economies. With evolution of Information Technology we first heard the Radio and later the TV that could capture pictures from the air and show it on the TV box. Then came the 'Computer' which was aptly the magic box. Computers and advancement of information and communication technology heralded the arrival of 'Internet' or 'World Wide Web' technology.

What a difference the Internet has made to our lives. No other invention has had such a mass transformational power over the entire human society, enterprise, business, economy as well as the political systems, education and the world communities and nations at large. The internet is rightly called the highway that has managed to erase the borders between countries and societies and taken the human society to a different level altogether.

Take a look at our lives today. There is no aspect of our life that is not interfaced with internet in one way or the other. From an individual's need to find a date or a suitable life partner to one's banking, insurance and other payments as well as dining out and not to forget the online shopping, internet has managed to become the mainstream facilitator to each and every individual.

Today millions of users access and use the internet for various purposes throughout the day. They use the internet for searching, browsing, writing & communication, listening, watching news, videos, publishing copying, printing, discussions, trading and selling etc. The list of activities and choices that the internet has got to offer to individuals is ever expanding. With millions of users actively looking for various products, information and services, there is a huge opportunity for the businesses to jump on to the internet bandwagon and cash in on the business opportunity that is presenting itself every minute.

Technology has helped build a platform that has enabled the businesses to cash in on the huge population and market that is now accessible over the internet and sell to them. Take the case of Online Banking, Mobile Banking, Debit| Credit Cards, ATMs as well as online trading and other business transactions, all these have grown and happened as a result of technological advancement in terms of communication, software as well as hardware technologies. From the time that one connected to Internet using a desktop, model and a telephone line to the Wi-Fi technology of today, we have graduated very fast making it possible to buy and sell at the click of a button. At another level the Business Processes as well as ERP coupled with various software and applications besides EDI, have enabled businesses to go 'On Line' with their business models.

Today no business, be it Business to Business or Business to Consumer, can ignore the huge 'Online Market' that exists on the internet. E Commerce was inevitable. Physical markets have literally been replaced with 'Virtual Markets'. E Commerce has had far reaching impact on business organisations for it has redefined 'Market'. E Commerce has made it possible for sellers to reach out to planet wide markets and consumers, thus changing the way business is conducted. For every prospective Management Professional, the in depth understanding of 'Online Marketing' and 'E Commerce' have become very important.

Marketing managers have got to go back to the class rooms to learn the new rules of game in handling Online Marketing which is drastically and totally different from the traditional marketing, selling, distribution and advertising strategies. Understanding all about Internet, E Commerce mechanisms, technologies, learning how to market online, understanding E Customer and learning to identify, build and nurture a relationship with the E Customer become the building blocks of one's new learning.

Basic Understanding of E-Commerce

Simply put, E Commerce is 'Using Electronic Platform for Business Transactions'. It is also called a 'Virtual Market Place'. Every minute millions of people from all over the world are logging into the Internet looking for some information, for product, services, to look for news, download music, for online shopping and so on. Every individual is looking for something that he would like to obtain or buy online instead of having to go through a physical transaction. Imagine what this means to the business organisations. If they are able to identify and access those individual users who have a specific need or want, they have a ready customer in waiting.

One could wonder whether it is the online community or the technology that is paving way for E Commerce. The answer is that both these factors are driving the E Commerce. The technological developments are providing the backbone for business transactions to take place and the growing volumes of users buying online is making it possible for E Commerce and markets to grow.

E Commerce is characterized by Business to Business and Business to Customer business models. We are very familiar with the Business to Customer model for banking; insurance as well as online shopping, online booking etc that have become very popular and accepted modes in our daily lives. On the B to B front too, business organisations have re-engineered their Business processes including Advertising, Marketing, Sales Order Management besides Supply chain management and Customer Relationship management to suit the E Commerce mode. Dell has successfully adapted 'online selling' model on a global scale. It allows the customers to 'configure the model' and to 'Order Online'. Once the transaction has been successfully carried out and payment has been received, Dell executes the order and ensures that the DELL Products are delivered at the Customer's door step within seven working days. DELL has not only used E Commerce successfully as its major selling channel, but at the backend they have put in place 'Built to Order' process where in the Computer is assembled against the specific customer order and is delivered to the customer. By integrating E Commerce and its Manufacturing process, DELL has managed to do away with holding inventories and managed to bring its costs down.

E Commerce has become a major business process for Global organisations and Multi National Companies. Most MNCs depend upon 'Online selling 'as well as 'Online Procurement' on global scale. E Commerce has made it possible for them to access global markets as well as source raw materials from across the world. Besides, E Commerce has brought down the cost of selling as well as cost of procurement drastically adding to the bottom line. In the consumer world, Insurance, banking, airlines and hospitality sectors have stood to benefit from E Commerce model of selling.

E Commerce is a reality. Several multiple technologies, platforms, agencies and networks make it possible for E Commerce to happen. EDI and Online banking and transactions have been the major enablers that have made it possible for business transactions to take place.

It is simply amazing to think that with the click of a button one can buy, sell or affect financial transactions worth millions of dollars in a few minutes. However this is true and E Commerce is the future.

Advantages of E-Commerce

We are living in the Information Age. Internet has changed our lives and these changes are irreversible. Slowly every home is being taken over by Internet. People have switched over to paying all their bills online, banking online and even shopping online. Internet is being used by people for various purposes. The more people get on to internet and search for information, the more opportunities begin to develop for e commerce.

Over the years internet has become the highway for

online business transactions. From Banks offering online banking to online bookings with airlines, hotels and travel to insurance sectors, all business to customer types of business have hitched on to the highway for accessing millions of customers through the internet. These are not the only businesses that are transacting via e commerce. Most of the large business houses have gone the E Commerce way to do online procurement as well as manage sales orders and Customer management. ERP systems have managed to integrate and bring online, all modules of business operations on web mode. Millions of dollars are being spent by business organisations in upgrading their IT infrastructure, Application platforms as well as re engineering their business processes to be able to get on to the highway of using E Commerce platform for their business operations.

There is no choice for businesses but to get on to the E Commerce way. At various levels from the simple mom and pop shop to the global corporations, all businesses have got to adapt to E Commerce for this is the way the future is going to be.

E commerce brings its own unique advantages and contribution to the businesses. First and foremost internet being a world wide web, opens up the world as a market to the businesses. Businesses can reach out to millions of customers in an instant which is not possible in any conventional mode of marketing. One of the most significant advantages that E Commerce offers is the cost. The cost of marketing online across the globe is miniscule when compared to the actual cost of marketing in the conventional ways. The cost per transaction works out to be very cheap. More over E Commerce promotes paperless offices and processes thus contributing to savings in terms of resources too. These and many more advantages make obvious business sense for Companies to market their products and services online.

In the last few years the speed of internet as well as the applications, software and hardware supporting E Commerce have developed and integrated to make E Commerce a real time business process. Online financial transaction capability has given a significant push to E Commerce. E commerce has not only caught the imagination of B to B and B to C businesses but today we have online trading which has perhaps changed the way stock markets, financial markets and commodity exchanges across the world function.

Today's customers are net savvy and know what they want. In essence today's customers are not willing to wait. No matter how good the product may be, speed is the essence here. From online shopping to online dating and searching for life partners, all of the individual's needs are being addressed by businesses via the web.

Looking at E Commerce from a marketing perspective brings the product or the service closer to the customer. It enables the customer to view, read, download and experience the product. The other significant difference from conventional marketing is that the online marketing enables the marketing company to customise its sales pitch or product offering to the customer. As against the conventional modes which target consumers and markets at large, with internet marketing and E Commerce it is possible to target every single individual making it more personalised and customised offer. E Commerce is just catching up. How

E Commerce will develop and grow and its future impact on the way business is carried on cannot be imagined and every business small or big has no choice but to jump on to the E Commerce bandwagon.

E Commerce - Changing Business Trends

Business Managers of today are living in challenging times. Business targets had never been stiffer, work pressure and managing the complexities of competition is keeping them on their toes all the time. Today, success or failure of a business and the Organisation is dependent wholly upon the Organisation's ability to be flexible and to respond to the external changing environment. Only those who are able to adapt to the changes and those who are able to assimilate and learn from tomorrow's technology are able to run the race. Digital technology has changed the rules of business game.

Today, individuals have the power of internet in their hands. If one wants to book an airline ticket, it is pretty easy to do so online and it takes only a few minutes to complete the entire transaction of looking at the options, selecting the best priced deal, making an online payment and printing the confirmed ticket. As compared to talking to a travel agent for an hour and several calls, online booking is definitely a better deal. Take the case of courier industry. One can book a consignment to any location in the world and you can use the track and trace feature on the web to track the status of your parcel at any time. This feature makes a huge impact to a business which is sending some important and time bound cargo or document to another location. Look at how easy it has become to configure a computer that you want and order it online in an instant.

From the above examples it is very clear that the businesses that have adapted and embraced E Business and E Commerce have managed to be successful and ahead in the industry. Migrating to an E Business environment is not easy and simple. It is not as simple as it looks that one can just buy an application and host it on the net and attract customers. Embracing e business calls for Organisations to change their business models, business strategies as well as integrate their business processes with technology.

Organisations were traditionally product oriented. With times and changing environment they grew to understand

and appreciate the need to be Customer centric and Customer relationship management became a key focus area. Being customer centric meant orienting the entire organisation and all its functions and divisions to be responsive to the internal and external customers. With the advent of E Commerce the Organisations have got to understand the Customers and their needs, preferences and buying behaviour in new light and from the perspective of electronic and digital media.

Understanding the why, how and what of E Commerce and orienting the entire Organisation to be customer centric in the new environment calls for re-inventing the business model where technology becomes the driver and the key differentiator. The entire Organisation needs to elevate itself and graduate to new web enabling platforms where speed, information, visibility and co-ordination of multiple transactions, seamless working of applications connecting different business processes form the components of the business chain.

Speed is the essence of E Business. Organisations have no time to learn all about the new technology, analyse, understand and then make their decision to embrace and grow into the E Business. Time and speed will either make or break the businesses today. Therefore the Managers and Management have got to work and migrate their businesses to the E Business platform at the speed of thought and it has got to be done now.

What, Why and How of E Business

For long Businesses and Organisations have been Customer oriented. They have moved from product and service mindset to Customer Satisfaction and Customer Delight mind set. The Customer expectation defined the marketing and business strategies of the Organisations. Organisations have begun to listen and tune in with the markets and customers to improve its product delivery and gain Customer relationship and loyalty. However in the new environment of the digital economy, they have to re learn all lessons with respect to the Customer behaviour. The challenge for the Organisations today is not only to tune into the markets and customers but to anticipate and estimate the Customer behaviour in the digital market place and be ready to service the customers in the new environment.

For all businesses, migrating to the new Net Economy is a necessity. Those Companies that have successfully managed to tune into the Customer on the internet have managed to be successful. Take the case of Dominos, Wal Mart, Amazon and EBay etc. What differentiates these businesses is that they have managed to grow their business models to suit the Customers who are using technology. Customer centric business models have been the hallmark of their success. The key differentiator can be said to be a combination of technology as well as Customer Centric business focus.

The key to E Business model is in understanding the Customer needs in the light of the new environment. Internet has changed a lot of dimensions for the individual users. Technology has changed the power equation from product and service to information and speed of information. In the new age of internet and online buying / selling, customers are not looking at the best product or service alone. In the virtual market where the competition, products and services are many, the information and the speed of information has become the key differentiator.

Take the case of couriers. The availability of Track and trace of a consignment that is provided by companies like DHL, FEDEX and UPS gives the power of information to the Customer enabling him to take key decisions with the help of the information on hand. Depending upon the urgency or the need of the hour, he can work with the courier company to change the delivery mode, uplift the consignment on urgent basis and meet with the delivery deadline of his customer. For flower exporters, fruit and perishable article exporters, such information can help deal with make or break situations.

E Marketing is significantly different from the traditional marketing. E Marketing with the help of technology and data warehousing is able to get to know and address the Customer on an individualized basis rather than one generic advertisement meant for the larger public. The companies are able to reach, recognize and customize the products and solutions to the specific individual customer.

Today's technology savvy customer is different from the traditional buyer. His buying behaviour as well as expectations are different. His demands are largely driven and enabled by the E Business technology with speed and information being critical to the buying process. The influencers and the buying process too have changed. Social media networks have emerged as the major influencers aiding the buyer's decision making process and online financial transactions mechanism too have changed the buyer's preferences and methods of buying. Understanding the new Customer behaviour and building a E Business as well as Marketing Strategy in this new environment is the challenge for every Marketing Manager.

Mapping Customer Behaviour and Pattern is the starting point of E Marketing

Learning all about E Commerce and E Marketing is the pressing need of every student as well as every marketing and business manager. No one can afford to ignore the E Business channel and hope to grow one's business the traditional way. Even if an Organisation continues to explore and grow its traditional channels of sales and distribution, the online presence is something that will need to be considered as a parallel marketing strategy, simply for the fact that the competition will be present and visible to the customer and more importantly the customer expects you to be available on the net.

The starting point of understanding all about E Business is to first understand and explore the Internet and its users.

Understanding of the user's profile, their habits and behaviour gives us an idea of the market and the characteristics of the customer group.

One needs to keep in mind that internet provides for some basic and unique features that make it attractive for the individuals to access the internet and search. The internet carries the power of providing information globally as well as instantly.

The amount of information and data available on the internet is so huge and varied that it makes the individual feel overwhelmed. Truly it takes the individual user on an information highway. With the realisation of this, an individual feels overawed and powerful at the same time. Internet browsing then becomes an exhilarating and liberating habit where in the customer gets used to shopping online and depending upon internet for his services.

Once there is an understanding of what internet is all about we see that individuals get into the habit of logging and browsing the internet for several hours a day. They may not have any specific need but like to make friends, participate in discussions and usually hangout. Researchers have carried out specific analysis and say that amongst the millions of users on the internet, most of them happen to be men who are not married but are professionals and students. From the profile of the users it is very evident that their needs of using internet have to do with looking for information, emailing, chatting and making friends. One basic need of every human being is the need to be in touch with others and communicate with other individuals. Internet makes this happen so easily and instantly that it makes the users engage in conversations and relationships without any inhibitions and thus become a part of virtual communities.

We also have the families who have internet at home and are used to using the internet for some online shopping and payment of their bills. Online banking has been accepted widely by everyone since the banks have managed to provide simple but secure transaction desks that has made it very convenient for the users. People have accepted and begun online shopping for a few of the things like books, furniture, clothes etc. While shopping too, individuals look for a familiarity with the Organisation that is front ending on the internet. Amazon, E Bay etc have become symbols of trust. Most people living in cities have begun to depend upon the internet for booking their movie tickets, ordering Pizza on home delivery as well as making their travel arrangements and downloading music and movies too.

One fact that stands out clearly is that people use internet mainly to search for information. Search holds the key to attracting the customer and getting him to check out what the business has got to offer. Second fact is that most internet users use internet not for buying but for browsing through virtual communities and checking out various information. This gives us the clue that the web pages have got to be compelling enough to get his attention. There is yet another fact that one might over look, which is that the number of users on the internet are a small fragment of the entire community and this number is growing every day. So who do all these mean to the marketing manager who is trying to map an E Marketing strategy for his business?.

Studying the behaviour and understanding the needs of the internet customers gives us an insight as to how to forge a relationship with customers via the internet and offer customised solutions. Internet customers today are looking for convenience of shopping and transacting easily and are also looking for the cheapest bargains as well as faster service and delivery too. These are the basic demands of every customer who will be going through your website. But then how will you stand out from amongst the competition and engage your customer into a relationship is the primary challenge in E Marketing.

E Commerce related Technologies

A layman using internet is overwhelmed by the sheer amount of information that he or she is able to access in an instant. Little do people know that the so called **information high way is a culmination of thousands of networks, multiple technologies, platforms, applications and**

programmes working together in co-ordination to deliver information to you and to enable a successful business transaction.

Getting into E Commerce is but inevitable for all business organisations. However designing a E Marketing strategy and setting up a the technical infrastructure to enable business transactions via the internet is not a simple task. It requires a thorough understanding of the technology environment, the pros and cons of using internet as well as implementing support structures and business processes that act as back up for E Commerce. This understanding is essential for the Management as well as the Marketing Managers who are the key planners of E Marketing strategies.

Most of the Organisations keep their E Commerce and internet related IT infrastructure separate from the internal Company servers and information. World Wide Web is truly an open high way where any information that is available on the server can be accessed by any one through search mechanisms. More over there are several tools available on the internet that can be used by hackers to steal information from your site, to divert traffic from your mail systems and play havoc with your website. Organisations would not wish to keep all information open to one and all. Several technologies such as intranet that hosts information and make it available to internally as well as authentication, data encryption and firewall technologies come into play as important and integral part of the IT design. Every day new methods of hacking, spreading virus etc are being introduced into the internet forcing the Organisations to continually monitor and upgrade their internet system security as well as transactional security and these calls for continual investments.

Internet technology environment is also dominated by the multi-media technologies as well as the evolving communication network technologies. Information is delivered to the customer using multi media using audio as well as video mode. Transmitting and reaching the information and content calls for the connectivity and hardware infrastructure technologies. We have seen the development of 2G, 3G,4G technologies available through cable, satellite, Wi-Fi modes connecting not only to the

Computers but to a host of other hand held devices such as mobile smart phones, tablets etc. Today the connectivity related infrastructure has merged voice| telephone, data as well as video and the service providers are vying with one another to dominate the end point serviceability to individual customers as integrated service providers.

In case of doing business via the internet be it exchanging mails, sending documents or affecting transactions, Several technologies like digital signature and other cryptographic protocols have to be employed to ensure authenticity as well as prevent any tampering etc. Authentication and validation process besides security checks form the basis of e business transactions. On the legal front too Organisations have got to watch out for issues concerning copy writes, licenses as well as intellectual property when it comes to their E Business and web sites.

Getting into E Business |Commerce calls for building trust with the customer. When there is a financial impact in any transaction and when it comes to an online financial transaction, the security and completion of transaction has got to be flawless. For the customer to be able to trust the

Company and agree to make online payment, the systems as well as the security checks and balances have got to be fool proof and need to be upgraded from time to time.

Understanding of the technology environment, knowledge of the threats, ability to build stronger systems, ensuring that the transactions and processes are legally compliant as well as tax compliant are the basics that have to be taken into account while designing E Marketing strategy. All these issues have got to be addressed by using technology products and third party suppliers.

Marketing managers not only face the challenge of having to understand the internet customer and his behaviour but have got to understand the technology environment, the threats and pitfalls along with compliance issues that exist. Technology element is one of the major components that have a bearing on the E Business strategy.

Search - Starting Point of Understanding for E Marketing Exercise

As a Marketing professional you are too familiar with marketing research. In fact Organisations spend millions of dollars into market research to know anything, everything and all things about their customers. The market research analysis and outcome becomes the input for developing Marketing, Advertising and selling strategies as well as in designing product strategy as well as supply chain and pricing strategies as well. So if you are now faced with the assignment of developing an E-advertising strategy and E Marketing strategy what is it that you have got to do?.The answer is very simple. You have got to start from the basics of getting to know all about your E-Customer.

If you map the actions of any individual customer who switches on his computer and connects to the internet, you will notice that there is one basic function that he happens to engage in. He begins to search for information and data. Therefore **search is the beginning and connecting link between your business and the customer**. Understanding all of the customer's search behaviour, understanding how the search happens through the search engines, the dynamics of searches is the first step.

This understanding will give you an idea of how to position your advertising and build your content in websites in such a way as to be able to be picked up by the Search engines and be ranked on top. Individuals normally look to the first two or three top ranking websites that come up in the searches. Therefore it becomes important to be able to position your website and advertising in such a way as to be amongst the top ranking sites.

Understanding all about the search trends provides you with a lot of market research and information on your potential customer and markets. From the searches that users conduct on the internet you are able to see the trends, look at the products and services that most customers are trying to look for and buy. Further you can also use the information gathered to build effective marketing communication that enables you to get closer to your customer. You are better positioned to speak customer's language for you know what exactly he has been searching for from the past data.

When the number of internet users is increasing daily, you have got to accept that your potential market is growing. You need to develop an effective search acquisition strategy to be able to reach out to this audience.

As the population all over the world is shifting their focus from reading magazines and print media and instead are concentrating on getting the same information from the internet, you will know that the time has come to re-design your advertising strategy and concentrate more on the internet -online advertising rather than on the print media.

The words and criteria that the individual users to search for information on the internet plays an important part in designing your advertising as well as entire website strategy. An individual might be looking for information on latest mobile phone but might search the internet by typing cell phone or smart phone or by a particular brand etc. This information when analysed gives us the clue to understanding customer's requirement, his thought process and the information he is seeking. It also helps us to build the advertising and web pages make them SEO optimized and in a way that ensures that it gets picked up by the search engine easily and is listed at the top.

The entire e-marketing exercise is built on the internet search. There are basically two types of searches namely Organic Search and Paid search. Organic search refers to the process that the search engines use to search for web pages, to rank the pages and list them using the algorithm that has been developed for its search function. Paid search on the other hand refer to the paid or sponsored advertisements that are picked up by search engines and listed as sponsored advertisements.

Furthermore one should also note that the offline advertisement can spill into the e advertisements and vice versa. The line between the two different platforms is narrowing. For effective design and delivery of advertisements and to be able to reach the customers first, you have got to be at the top of the list when the customer is searching. Understanding all about searches then is the first step in developing E Marketing and E Advertisement plan.

Search Engines and SE Marketing

Internet is not something that is alien technology anymore. Every home and every individual has adapted to using internet for various purposes. It has become a habit for everyone to use the internet to search for all kinds of information. Searching happens to be the main feature or the tool with which one gets across the internet. If you are a marketing manager or a business manager, When millions of individuals are using the internet and searching for products and information etc, you have got to be able to identify and reach out to those who are looking for the products and services that you are offering and get across to them. If the users are using Search Engines to look for information, it is only right that you should know all about how Search Engines work and function to be able to build a relevant strategy to reach out to the prospective Customers.

You might be familiar with the often used Search Engines like Google, Yahoo, AOL etc. When you type in the keywords for the information that you are searching for, the Search Engine uses the keyword as the criteria to search through the web pages and all directories as well as databases and lists the websites by choosing the relevance of information as per the keyword.

Search Engines use crawlers or spiders which go through the contents of web pages, index them as per the relevance and within seconds publish the list of websites for you to choose from.

If you look at this process from the point of a marketing person you will realise that you need to build a advertising strategy whereby you are positioning your web pages in a manner that the Search Engine is able to easily pick your website and show it up right within the first few top ranking links in the list. The webmaster is the expert who will help you build the web page with the right kind of Search Engine Optimization. In simple terms, the Web master researches to find out the Most Frequently researched words relevant to your product on the Search Engines and helps design the web page content and design using these key words as well as links. The search process and algorithm used by the Search Engines carry vary from one SE to another from time to time.

The Web Master keep a track of the evolving designs and build their web pages| alter the contents accordingly to suit the SEO. This design strategy is a part of Search Engine Marketing Strategy. By increasing the relevance of the web pages, you can increase the traffic into your website. Web Masters also employ several other methods of link farming, reverse linking etc to divert traffic into your website. The concept here may be considered to be similar to that of cold calling or prospecting. With the increase in number of visitors to your website or to paid advertisement, you can hope to convert a percentage of prospective visitors as customers.

Apart from Search Engine Optimization, effective content and online advertising plays a major part in getting the attention of the prospective customer. Unlike the print and other visual media, the cost of online advertising works out to be way cheaper and effective too. The art of prospecting a customer, pre selling and converting a prospect to a sale is different from the conventional method. Understanding of the medium, understanding of the customer's buying behaviour and the other dynamics of internet sales has to be understood thoroughly to be able to design an effective E- Marketing Plan for your business| product.

SEO and Search Engine Marketing Processes

If you are in the process of understanding and designing an E Marketing strategy for your business, understanding and learning all about Search Engine Optimization becomes necessary. You will need to look for and hire a reliable, experienced and dependable SEO Company who will design your web pages, build the online advertising as well as help build traffic into your website and incorporate the Customer Selling process.

Search Engine processes including both paid search and organic search is a highly dynamic field where new methods are being developed every day and new marketing campaigns as well as processes are being introduced in the market.

Therefore it is important to be able to choose the right SEO partner who is always ahead in the race and is able to keep ahead of the market developments and offer all of the SEO services under one roof.

A typical Search Engine Optimization Service plan starts first with analysing the keywords that are relevant to your product, service or business. A detailed research and analysis goes into making of a list of keywords that are most frequently searched for by the users and the variants of the key words that are often used. The second part of the plan involves researching and understanding the competition, understanding the market, the tactics and strategies used by the competition etc, to be able to build an effective counter strategy that can beat competition. The third step consists of designing the web pages including the web titles and meta - tags along with the optimized layout and structure that is Search Engine and indexing friendly.

There are several ways that you can check the validity of the keywords that have been used in your website. Using keyword selector tools such as Yahoo Keyword Selector, Google Keyword Selector or Google Trends, the content can be tested. Further on the SEO service provider works to build the links using partnerships as well as link building and publishing in the blogs, wiki as well as in all relevant video and audio sites. Submitting the website to number of search engines, directories to ensure that it is indexed and considered to be relevant is an ongoing job that is handled by the SEO experts. One other important function that is involved in the SEO Service plan is to monitor, evaluate and analyze the popularity and performance of the web site. There are several tracking soft wares that are available.

Search Engine Marketing involves usage of both Organic as well as paid search results. Paid search results include pay per click and other sponsored advertisement usage as well as paid listing, where in with one click the potential customer is able to access your company website directly. Besides these there are also the article submissions, submissions to blogs, press releases and other promotional works carried out by the SEO Experts to increase the popularity of the website.

Going forward the SEO experts also engage in Social Media Marketing tactics to attract and generate potential customers from amongst the internet users. Using Social Media Marketing does call for expertise for it involves influencing and building a community and influencing the users in their decision regarding their preferences for your products.

SEO & SEM activities are to be carried out continually adapting to the new changes in technology as well as tuning into the new trends and methods from time to time.

Search Data Helps Your Product and E-Marketing Strategy

Building an E Marketing plan for any business or product is quite engaging and challenging. What makes it more interesting is the fact that unlike traditional channels where one needs to depend upon market surveys and other means to gauge the customer behaviour, using the internet search data one can have instant feedback about the customer and this data can then be analyzed and used for building product strategy as well as marketing strategy.

Search is the basic tool that links customers to the product and to the seller on the internet. The search engines have built in processes and algorithms to identify, collect data and work on the data of the search words used by the millions of internet users. Most often the search words are limited to one or maximum of three words. The variations and the words used by the searchers may vary but will still be relevant to one subject. If you take an example of Americans and Canadians looking to migrate to Mexico for retirement, you will find that there are several thousand hits on words like 'Migrate to Mexico', 'Expat heaven in Mexico' and Retirement in Mexico' etc.

The search engines capture and analyze all the data and are built to prompt words to the users. When one types a few letters, the search engine prompts the rest of the options, which shows that the search engine has the data on the most sought after information on the internet and in the area that one is looking at.

The search data can be extrapolated to yield a variety of information about the Consumer behaviour. The data can be analyzed to understand what exactly the customer's intent is, what exactly the prospective customer is looking for and more details about how many customers are looking for the same information, the geographical location of the searchers etc. All of these details generated can be and are being used by companies and incorporated to build better products and services that the customers are looking for and also to build the exact fit. Take the case of accommodation during summer in UK. From the search information data of the millions of users who search for specific information about accommodation in UK, very many details regarding the exact location, the type and size of accommodation as well as the budget and other requirements can be tabulated. The number of prospective customers can also be mapped location wise. Such kind of detailed analysis can help a tour operator to custom build products that suit the customers keeping in line with the findings. In case of car sales, the Car manufacturing company can get to see who and how many are looking for what kinds of cars, what are their specific requirements in terms of priority be it with safety features, the speed, the mileage or the cost etc. Besides, the marketing communication can also be targeted at the specific customer group making it more specific and customised to attract attention. The data helps build customer specific and one to one marketing communication. All of the marketing and branding exercise can be done at costs that are miniscule compared to the traditional media advertising.

Keeping in line with changing lifestyle and economics, the customer behaviour is varying and changing. This can also be tracked easily using the search data and depending upon the report; product and services can be modified or suited to meet the new requirements. Besides, the data gathered about the consumer behaviour can also be used to build the marketing strategy for the traditional channels too.

The search data gives you a lot of insight into your customer, his background, his habits, preferences as well as his buying behaviour. It also provides a picture about the competition too. The size of the market, the sensitivities of the market and consumer, provide the marketer with specific information that can help in building products and services which match with the customer expectation and one can look at means and ways to beat competition too. If the customer is looking for 'Cheapest' and not necessarily the 'Best', you know how you have got to position your product to such customer.

SEO Optimization is a part of the E Marketing plan that uses the search data and the key word to build relevant links and website content and to attract the customer. This apart, the marketing managers find the search data to be a gold mine that gives them complete insight into the customer and helps build the product, pricing, promotion and distribution strategies to suit the customer needs.

E Business Needs E Organization

We are living in exciting times. Technology is making unprecedented advancements affecting all walks of life. New Economy and new technology have paved way for new ways of business namely E Commerce. Businesses are under intense pressure to perform in the market place and are vying for space amongst competitors. While the managements are under constant pressure to meet new revenue targets they are also under pressure to add to the bottom lines and reduce costs. E Business has come in at the right time to help companies explore new channel, new markets, to beat competition as well as cut down the costs. Companies that sell their products and services and provide customer service online have managed to beat competition successfully and take the lead.

Dell is one such early adaptors of technology who took the lead in offering Direct Selling option using internet. Competition in the Computer Desktop and Laptop market is very intense with all of the big names like IBM, Lenovo, HP etc. The margins too are very thin owing to the fact that the prices are falling and the technology is changing every few years. In such intense price sensitive market, the pressure to keep costs under control is always increasing. Dell's direct selling model has been a huge success right from the time that they started selling online.

Getting into E Business is not a simple process of setting up a website and enabling online transactions. There is more to it that just using the internet and technology to book orders. E Business calls for building a new business structure in the Company that includes the entire Organisation. Forward and backward integration will need to be in place. All of the business functions in the Organisations would need to be integrated and shifted to Enterprise technology or ERP platform with seamless integration.

While order management and financial transaction reconciliation is important as far as the e sales is concerned, the backend supply chain would need to be equipped to manage the entire process from manufacturing to delivery to the customer's doorstep within the committed time. The manufacturing or assembly is carried out in one location while the customer might be located in another country or region. Such integration of manufacturing, supply chain and deliveries cannot be managed by the Company alone. It calls for collaboration and partnership with several partners and service providers along the value chain. It also calls for establishing and integrating processes, technology, trained manpower and focus as well as dedication of managements and relationships across all channel partners to ensure smooth flow of information as well as physical products. In case of Dell, the raw material and component supplies are housed next to the assembly plant by a third party service provider on behalf of the DELL vendors.

VMI or Vendor Managed Inventory ensures that Dell gets the supplies of raw materials immediately upon request at its plant and Dell does not own any inventories. Once the assembly is completed, a third party service provider picks up the consignment, stores it at the warehouse, ships it to the destination after completing all documentation and formalities. At the destination the agent or another third party service provider partner picks up the consignment for onward delivery to the Customer at his door step and finally uploads the delivery confirmation into Dell's tracking website. All through the chain, host of service providers are engaged and systems and processes are relied upon to track, manage and control the shipments and deliveries at all times.

The entire E Business program calls for establishing and integrating technology as the business driver and leveraging on technology to deliver superior delivery service beating competition. Such a business endeavour calls for establishing a new business model that is tuned to and working on E Business model.

What is Online Advertising - A Basic Understanding

Marketing managers are brushing up their marketing lessons, for the world and markets have changed with E Commerce. The traditional theories are no longer relevant and sufficient, for people have now begun to switch over to online buying. Of course as compared to the traditional ways of buying goods, online shopping is but a small percentage of the total trade. However over the years the trend of online shopping is increasing and in the years to come it is certainly going to catch up and grow faster.

Companies are fast realizing the need to have an E Marketing plan. Whether the Organisation chooses to offer online business to its customers or chooses to continue with existing channels of sale, the fact remains that one does not have an option but to be present on the web. When a customer is looking for information concerning the particular product or business that the Organisation is engaged with, it is important that the Organisation or brand be represented and feature amongst the list when searched and looked upon by the customers.

Organisations big or small need to have their presence felt in the web. Going by the simple logic, if your customers are on the internet, then your Organisation has got to be on the internet too. In other words we can very well say that businesses do not have a choice but to be in the place where the customers are.

While working out a strategy or marketing plan, a lot of focus is paid to the advertising and business promotions strategy. In the current scenario, **there is a need to integrate the e-advertising along with conventional advertising**. Again whether the Company proposes to sell online or not, advertising the latest products and being in news becomes a necessity. There arises a need to work out the advertising and promotional plan in detail, including the traditional media as well as the internet media and see how to synchronize all the mediums to get the best results. The present trend followed by general public seems to be that they watch the advertisements through various mediums such as TV, Print Advertisements etc and for further information they tend to visit the Company Website for more details. Whoever is on the internet inadvertently tends to use the internet for further information on the subject of his or her interest. Therefore in the case of businesses running major advertising campaigns using other media will need to be advertising even on the internet at the same time and offer more product and sales information online.

If a Car Company is introducing a new model in the market, it is not enough to have the news splashed with all details on the news paper. People who are looking to buy a new car are likely to see the advertisement on the newspaper but immediately check out the internet to see more details. In such cases, it helps to have all details about the car being made available on the website. All those who visit the website to have a look at the car are the prospective customers. The marketing can pick up and develop these leads further. There needs to be an option for the interested customers to initiate a sales request or some such process by which the customer can be engaged for further discussion.

It helps the Managers to think through and understand the concept of advertising on the internet and compare it with the traditional modes. Online advertising can provide a lot of information about the customer behaviour, his requirement and his feedback besides being able to quantify the market size and other characteristics of the market too.

To sum it up, Organisations have got to recognize and adapt online advertising as a part of overall advertising and promotional campaign. Understanding of online advertising, its effectiveness, its reach and the output from such online advertising is necessary for the decision makers to be able to build their Marketing strategies.

Paid Or Organic Search ?

Most Business Organisations both big and small have realised the necessity of having a presence on the internet.

Many Organisations limit themselves to setting up a Company website and provide contact information. Those who realise the potential of being able to tap the customers online go one step forward and provide online services. Whether the Organisation wishes to offer online sales or not, one of the basic marketing necessities vital for the business is the presence on the internet. When prospective customers are looking for products and services and when your competitors are present on the internet, do you have any option but to be advertising on the internet?.

Once the need for advertising on the internet has been established, the next relevant question that comes up is to choose between paid search or organic search for advertising. The technical aspects of development of the content and the website etc will be handled by the SEO specialists. However the marketing managers and the management need to understand some of the basic concepts that are relevant for their decision making and marketing plans.

Paid search as the word denotes, refers to online advertisements that are sponsored or paid for by the

Company. These sponsored ads are displayed along with the organic search results. The paid ads are built around specific target queries related to the product or the service that the Advertiser is trying to sell. These advertisements are retained only such time that the Company pays for each click. Organic search ads on the other hand refer to the list of websites or results that are put forth by the search engines. On receipt of a query, the search engines use certain algorithms to search for thousands of web pages using the key words as given in the query, list out the web pages in the order of relevance of the content to the query and publish the same. If you are the Marketing Manager, it is but natural that you are required to take a decision of choosing the Organic search option or the Paid search option. Making the right decision calls for understanding both options in detail.

Paid search advertising is generally built for a specific target audience. It caters to specific queries only. Since these are paid on per click basis, the effectiveness and viewership of these advertisements can be measured. More over the Marketing Manager can have a direct control over how much is being spent on the paid search advertising for it is paid on per click basis. It is also likely that the viewers who click on the advertisement and visit the web page are serious buyers and the chances of conversion into sales in such cases is very high.

Organic search on the other hand does not involve any payments and is hence long lasting. The effectiveness of the Organic advertising is dependent upon the Content of the website provided and the SEO optimization.

As long as the website gets listed on top of the list the viewers are likely to visit the website. The content displayed will determine whether it manages to get the viewer to be interested in contacting the Company and furthering his business interest or not. In this case the quality of the content will also signify the value proposition to the viewer. It is highly effective in engaging the customer and providing him value in terms of information. This mode helps build the brand image of the Company in the long run.

In the long run the Organic search has been found to be more effective than paid search advertising. The data analysis shows that the percentage of people looking through the websites that are listed through the Organic search is much more than the percentage that visits the paid advertisements. Paid search advertising can also be a highly effective option in case of short term sales campaigns and schemes that need high visibility and buzz.

Customer Expectation as Key Driver to Online Marketing Business

Internet is changing the customer's expectations as well as behaviour. Understanding the customer behaviour pattern holds the key to successful online business for Companies. Companies have begun to realise that the product as well as marketing strategies that work for traditional sales channels o not hold good for their E Commerce business models. We now see that Organisations are slowly moving away from focussing on product technology, production efficiency as well as cost reduction strategies and getting to understand their product delivery and services from the E Customer's perspective. E Customer's perspectives are forcing the E Commerce companies to change the value proposition of their business. The Customer's perception of value is what holds good in the E Commerce scenario and the Companies have got to re engineer their business strategies as well as functions in line to deliver the so called 'Value Innovation'.

If you look at the internet scenario, you will notice that the availability and reach of the competitors to the prospective customer's is easier and the e market is crowded with competitors. How big or small, how old or new these organisations are, doesn't matter to the prospective customer. What the customer is looking for is largely determined by his domestic situation.

Generally speaking, **all customers who are browsing the internet looking to make a purchase are looking to finish with the purchase immediately due to lack of time**. The time and speed as well as convenience of the e business model is what is prompting them to opt for online purchase. The next criterion that drives the customer to buy online is the fact that they are able to quickly check out the rates amongst competition and go for the cheapest deal. At this stage the quality of the product or service is already taken for granted that it is expected to be nothing but the best. The other factor that helps the customer go for the 'click' perhaps is the familiarity of the brand. In such a scenario, companies have no option but to keep ahead of the game by innovating and using technology and come out with 'value perception' schemes.

If you try to recall some of the most familiar names and brands on the internet the names like Google, Yahoo, Microsoft, AOL, Amazon, EBay etc come to one's mind easily. These companies have successfully engineered themselves to get closer to the customer and to provide the value perception. Mac Donald's have successfully built a brand internationally, a brand that promises certain quality and Customer experience. You get to see the One Dollar Store, No Frills flying and Daily lower prices by the retail giants having become popular with customers who feel happy with the value proposition.

Amazon.com has been hugely successful in using technology to deliver as well as exceed customer expectation in terms of value proposition and customer experience. The story of Amazon.com has become a case study with all business management courses. Amazon has become an online business giant within a short span of time beating their rivals and continue to grow exponentially year on year. The reason for the success lies in understanding the Customer Expectation and using Technology to build and deliver value proposition to customers and achieve Customer delight. They have invested extensively into building e mail infrastructure that has made it an easy, pleasant and interesting to look for books as well as compare and buy them online. Having added rich features of providing previews, press releases as well as by introducing the authors to the customers through the interviews, they have exceeded customer expectation and changed the value proposition for the customer. Customer gets tangible value in terms of free shipping, availability of used and second hand books and many more add on benefits when he chooses to buy more from the online store. Innovation is not only limited to the normal online transactions alone.

Amazon makes it a point to listen to the customers and try to offer customized solutions. The customer looking for any particular book that is out of print or not available in inventory can contact the Customer service who will try and arrange for the specific book from the publishers or suppliers as the case may be. These innovations have made them the leaders in their field and has won customer loyalty. Amazon's customers are not the same as those who would buy from any book store.

The geographic spread of the customers is across nations and international sales happy to hold a major share in its total sales, which means Amazon needs to have end to end service capability across all countries to be able to effect deliveries to the customer at his door step. Innovation, building back end capabilities and continuing to listen to the Customer and pre-empting his requirements for the future are the drivers that help with the Company's business strategy.

Getting To Know the Technicalities of Online Business

Getting to know all about E Marketing and how business is transacted online is important for every student of business management as well as for professionals. Online selling is picking up and growing. More and more people are beginning to find it convenient to shop online. With robust systems for financial transactions in place, consumers are beginning to gain confidence in shopping online and making payments.

Understanding all about E marketing begins with understanding how the internet works, how the customers search for information and data. Further on you will need to know all about how Search Engines work, how they gather the data by going through thousands of web pages, filter the content and produce the list of relevant websites within a matter of few seconds. From there on you will need to learn all about building web pages with SEO content and other technical features that will ensure that the traffic is directed to the website. Your website therefore is your identity on the internet.

You will need to understand all of the technicalities that go into building web pages, hosting the same as well as ensuring that the web page is so constructed and managed that it continues to be one of the top listed references. No doubt the technical aspects of web page hosting is the domain of SEO experts. But then as marketing or business managers, it helps to know the relevant details of how things work in this scenario so that you are in a position to work better with the developers and add value.

Websites will need to be continually upgraded with content as well as functionality. Sometimes the changes in marketing or selling strategy, changes in the business structure or the Company in terms of mergers etc or the changing technology environment might warrant changes to the website functionalities. In line with the communication strategy the website might need to go through periodic changes too. On the other front the site has to be continually upgraded to ensure better search ability too. Understanding these technical issues will help you identify problems as well as solutions that you might encounter in building your online sales model.

Search engines mine the data from thousands of web pages using sequential processes known as crawling, indexing and ranking. Sometimes the website architecture may not be sufficiently geared up to allow the search engines to extract the required data from the web pages easily and hence your site may not be getting listed right at the top of the list and you might be missing out on all those customers who are looking for making their online purchases right now. Technical glitches like slow server response time or page loading time can cause the search engine to skip your website and go forward. Several shortcomings in the content of the website can also contribute to the reason why your website might be figuring at the bottom of the list. Apart from non SEO Optimized content, there can also be problems with site registration that obstructs the search engine from accessing data from the web pages. There can be several issues with Java script and flash that can obstruct easy retrieval of content by the search engines. If your website content has too much of multi media objects with very less of extractable data or text, your web page may be easily by passed by the Search Engine.

Understanding some of the common technical issues related to website and content can help you work with the technical developers and come up with solutions that help in ensuring that your online business is on the right track towards progress.

Establishing Business Goals and Measurement is Necessary Before Embarking on E Marketing Implementation

Setting up a web page and promoting online business has become a necessity for all business organisations, irrespective of the size of the organisation and the business. Every minute, several thousands of people from all over the world are accessing the internet and searching for products and information. A few hundred of them could be looking for the product or service that you are marketing. This means you have got to be available and also be the first to reach out to such customers. If your competition has already set shop on the internet, do you have a choice but to follow suit?. Therefore the need for an E marketing strategy and business plan is easily accepted and embraced by the managements of all Business Organisations.

As you begin the process of working out the details of how, what, when and why of Online marketing, you will need to come up with the communication and promotional plan as well as the budget too. It is important to build an online marketing expense budget. This alone would not suffice when you submit the same to the management for approval. You will need to answer quite a few questions posed by management and the big bosses. To be able to answer the questions, you will need to work out a detailed plan of how to measure the performance, benchmark the performance of the website etc. Management function also involves having to gather, analyse and assimilate data to facilitate right decision making and achieving the business objectives.

The SEO company that you engage to build, host and manage your website will be able to offer you a list of reports with the frequency as desired by you. Number of reports such as ranking report, indexing, traffic report and many of other related reports can be made easily available. But these technical reports can hardly add value until and unless you have worked on the requirement of data as needed by the various business groups of your organisation.

Through the reports you will be able to understand your customer behaviour, expectations and get to know your customer better. You can get to know about your customer's requirement in specific which can be of great value to your product division which will be able to customise the product to suit the market needs. Sales department gets to benefit from knowing when, how and what the customer is going to buy and thus find ways and means to convert the prospect to a sale. Customer relationship management department will find the data very useful for it helps to manage the customer expectation, build relationship as well as loyalty. Marketing communication department would want to know the effectiveness of the online communication, as well as details of viewership etc. Further strategies of integrating TV and print media and conducting promotional sales campaigns as well as new product launches etc can be planned based using the data reports.

Finally, when the management decides to invest into the E marketing plan, it is important to identify and state the business goals, list the achievable targets and metrics to assess performance. Such clarity helps in building and implementing the online marketing strategy.

Online Sales Promotions and Advertising Methods

Sales Promotion and Advertising is one of the major activities of any Marketing Function in any business. Sales promotion and advertising is always drawn up based on the sales strategy combined with the nature and composition of the market. Audio, visual, print media advertising besides sales promotional campaigns have been the normal set of activities that go with marketing. When it comes to the E Marketing strategy, the need for online advertising remains the same as it is for the conventional sales. What is different from the traditional modes of sales promotion is that the methodology or the process adapted in the e world is different.

When you engage an SEO company to build a website for your, the developers take care to design the website, pages and the content, host, ensure it is listed as the top ranking page in any search and do all things necessary to get the traffic into website. To be able to attract the target audience and to connect with them, you will need to engage in online promotional activities. There are several types of online promotional activities that you can try out. One of the most popular ways of getting into online promotion is by using 'Online Ad Banners'.

When you surf on the net what strikes you and attracts your attention is the online banner. There are many more promotional activities like Internet newsgroups, Email broadcasts, Social Media Networking, Internet mailing list, sponsorship of online chats, electronic press release distribution etc. You can opt for free advertising as well as for paid advertising on the internet depending upon your choice of activity.

Advertising online using banners is one of the most popular methods. The banner space can be bought on the major search engines. Ad space can be bought on 'Pay per Click' method which makes it cost economical. Banners are also traded by many of the websites who exchange the banner space with other websites in their network. The banners would need to be catchy and attractive enough to make the customer to click and visit your Company website.

Blogs, News Groups and Mailing lists are also the favourite promotional activities adapted by the various brands. Blogs create a community of likeminded people and indirectly promote the products and services by building brand awareness and building a buzz around the products.

News groups and mailing lists involve posting messages about the chosen topics to the interested groups.

Using mailing lists you can reach out to your customers with customized messages and communication. You can broadcast your newsletters; keep your prospective customers informed of the sales promotions and online fliers too. New product announcements and offering new discounts and exclusive previews etc. Several search providers build mailing directories and provide services of distributing promotional materials and emails for clients. Soft wares are also used to build mailing lists and directories of email addresses and interested users.

Most of the interest users are used to receiving 'spam' mails. For some it has become a hate word too. Spam is a method of sending mails to millions of people using electronic mailing list. This is purely unsolicited mails. Such spam mails flood the inbox of users who find it a bother to go through unsolicited mails and happen to delete the mails without going through them. But then if the information is presented in a very interesting way and it manages to catch the attention of the users, the purpose of the mails will be successful. When compared to other modes of online promotions, this method turns out to be the most cost effective way.

E Commerce Trends

If internet has had far reaching impact on all walks of life, E trade has had similar impact on all types of businesses. No Organisation big or small, whether a global organisation or an individual owned enterprise can afford to ignore e commerce and e marketing scene. Normally we see people using internet to make their travel bookings like booking airline tickets online, make hotel reservations, look at the places of interest etc. People have also begun to shop online and buy fashion stuff as well as books and other items of interest.

Online buying has not been restricted to these alone. You may be surprised to know that cars are being bought online by customers. This new trend has had the car dealers as well as manufacturers to sit up and take notice of the changes in the buyer's behaviour. Internet is one medium that transfers the power of information to the users.

In the case of buying a car, the process of buying is heavily dependent upon information. **The fact that internet is able to provide detailed information, comparison and all details in the interactive and multimedia mode, customers find it very easy to surf the net for information about the cars.** Comparing specifications, models, and technical specs is easier on the internet for retrieving all the information about various brands can be done by the click of a button. It takes a few minutes to obtain all the information that one is looking for. Normally this process would have taken several weeks for the interested individual to compile information. Besides the price of the car, there are several other factors that go into the purchase of a car. In the buying process, car financing, warranty as well as insurance happen to be the major determinants too.

It would be interesting to see how auto sales have taken the e-commerce route. Check out the Auto By Tel website that offers a comprehensive solution to the customers to buy the car of their choice. This is not a dealer website but works like an exchange which has tied up with dealers, insurance agencies as well as accessory suppliers and other related vendors. Kelley Blue Book and Edmunds.com provide the individuals with the pricing information for each and every model of car in the market. It allows individuals to do their research, compare prices and models to arrive at their chosen car. Then all one needs to do is to fill up the detailed form online and register with Auto By Tel. The exchange then contacts the relevant dealers in the particular area and obtains the best quotes for the car, for insurance as well as the financing schemes, allowing the individual to select the best bargain.

The fact that people are buying cars on through this website shows that the purchasing behaviour and preferences of customers is changing. E commerce is providing them the alternatives. This poses the question to the car dealers as well as the manufacturers about the future of their business models. They have got to take time to understand the internet savvy customers, their behaviour, their concept of value and re design the marketing strategies. This change calls for re-engineering the entire business organisation towards E marketing and Online Selling.

Architects of E-Marketing Strategy

Shopping online has become a fashion statement with most people. Be it convenience or fad, thousands of people are learning to buy products and services online. Online shopping is not restricted to B to C segment alone. B to B segment happens to be larger than B to C and the transactions carried on are of much higher value. However online banking, online insurance, travel booking and buying books, music and CD etc happen to be the most favourite and often used services by people.

When you look at any business or industry vertical you will find that the product lifespan is shortening, consumer behaviour is changing so also is the business Organisation changing. To keep up with the changes be it in the market or technology, organisations are slowing beginning to understand and accept the reality that change is the only permanent solution. How fast an organisation is able to change and adapt to the new environment will determine how well it will perform in the market. Technology is the architecture of every business Organisation today. Embracing, investing and integrating technology has become inevitable. The CTOs of the Company are partnering with the Managements in guiding the future of the Organisation.

Today's CTOs have major strategic responsibilities in the Organisation. They are required to scan the environment, analyse the future trends and equip the IT architecture of the Business Organisation to be able to survive and perform well in the years to come. Especially in the case of E Business, the CTOs have got to ensure that the backend enterprise architecture is able to deliver the business performance.

E Commerce model demands immediate business delivery on the part of the Organisation. This is possible only when the business is built on and integrated using ERP applications.

IT applications supporting E Commerce models have got to be integrated seamlessly with the internal ERP systems as well as the third party systems that have been bundled together to facilitate seamless transactions. Any problem faced by customers in any of the online transactions, be it caused due to the system failure from the

Company or from the third party service provider, could result in loss of confidence in the Company and resultant loss of business as well as risk of damaging one's reputation.

Amazon has managed to score phenomenal success in its online selling business. They have managed to provide seamless process for the online buyers. Further, the online buying experience and satisfaction is enhanced by providing prompt and immediate deliveries which ensures customer loyalty and retention. To back up the online sales module, Amazon has set up equally efficient Order management and fulfilment systems coupled with physical infrastructure in terms of setting up warehouses in strategic locations, holding and managing inventories, fast and accurate operations in terms of order picks and despatch. The inventories of the warehouse are integrated with the Order management applications as well as the third party transport| courier service providers. Thus from the point of sale to order processing, inventory, shipment, tracking as well as POD recovery, systems drive the processes. This is not all; online payment is supported by third party bank that provides financial transaction support. All these and many more systems and IT architecture makes up for the Online Sales model of Amazon a runaway success.

E Marketing or E Commerce strategy therefore needs to involve the active participation and ownership not only from the Management and Marketing but also the IT |Technical teams too. It is the IT teams who become the principle architects of designing and implementing the E marketing strategy of the Company.

Dynamics of E-Selling - A Perspective

Internet has ushered in the information age. Explosion of information, speed of information retrieval has changed the thinking process of individuals. Similarly online business too has had far reaching effect on consumers. Convenience, time, effort, resource saving coupled with ease of transactions is driving online business to newer heights. Man is a creature of habits and comforts. These two basic factors will fuel online business in the times to come.

Organisations and businesses have got to understand this factor and appreciate the inevitability of linking their products and services to this engine called E Commerce.

Online selling is going to be the engine driving the businesses in future.

Adapting E Commerce benefits both the Organisation as well as the Customer. Organisations need to keep finding new markets and new customers to ensure they grow. This means covering new geographical territories.

Engaging new customers requires efforts in carrying out the pre sale process. When it comes to managing huge volumes of transactions, as well as with limitations in the traditional selling methods, the sales processes gets tougher. Humanly it becomes difficult to provide quality pre sales and marketing services to a huge market and court potential customers effectively. In case of E Business the concept of geographical boundaries as well as availability of information have no limitations. Understanding these dynamics, the service sector businesses like airlines, travel, real estate, finance, insurance etc have quickly moved to E Commerce platform and benefitted from the use of technology.

Acquisition of new businesses, products and mergers have become the vehicle for growth and expansion of business organisations. Marrying two diverse cultures, products and synching them into a new format, can be a huge challenge as well as crucial for the survival. Adapting E platform at this juncture has proved to be the engine for success with most Organisations. Electronic commerce platform has enabled the new business units to expand their market reach and provide several products and services to the customer under one brand umbrella. Take the case of any financial services bank or company. They offer in addition to private banking, commercial lending, home mortgage, fixed deposits, wealth and portfolio management services, money transfer, mutual funds and access to stock markets, trading as well as insurance and related products. Using E technology, the Organisation is able to provide systematic and consistency in service delivery in a transparent and speedy manner. Standardization of systems and processes enables the Organisation to upgrade its service levels irrespective of the size of the customer base besides providing transparency in its transactions. The use of processes and e platform helps build the brand image too.

Looking at the Customer's point of view, e platform facilitates availability of information at finger tips. Information is the key to the Customer's decision making process. Using internet, customer can download all the information about product, competition, as well as compare the pricing and do all of the homework that he would need to do to arrive at a decision comfortably without having to move out of his home or office. The information is all available at the click of a button. Let us look at the other factors that play an important role in his decision to go ahead and buy. Typically the customer looks to cheapest but the best product besides looking for the fastest delivery times. Again referring back to the banking sector, the companies offer the best products at very competitive rates for the competition pressure successfully keeps the pricing on a tight leash. The customer is able to check out the prices across competition easily.

With all things being equal, the differentiating factor for the customer to make a decision in favour of a particular company would be the brand image and the online service capability of the business Organisation. Once the customer is used to and is ready to make his purchase online, he is essentially expecting a hassle free transaction, a speedy transparency of process. All these translate to the online service features and capabilities that have been built into the website. The quality of the online service including the website attractiveness, features, speed and safety play a vital role in engaging the customer positively. The customer who is confident in a particular brand or is confident about the online website and the transactions of a particular organisation would ultimately choose to go and make his purchase online. Especially in the case of service industry, the deliverables and the visibility created on the website conveys the service capability of the Organisation in the absence of human interaction.

Understanding the different aspects and dynamics of the E commerce helps the business managers to appreciate and adapt to the emerging scenarios and make the business as well as professional transition smoothly.

E Marketing and Customer Relationship Management - Two sides of the same coin

Whenever one talks of E marketing strategy or plan, they normally include online selling, online promotions and advertising. However this could be a very narrow view or definition as applied to E marketing. Planning for Customer Relationship Management is as important as paying attention to online selling efforts.

Let us look at understanding some of the consumer trends and behaviour and apply it to the E Commerce platform. Every marketing professional and businessman knows that selling to a repeat buyer or an already existing customer is far easier than the effort required in developing a new customer. Secondly the cost of selling to an existing customer can be only 15% of the cost of selling to a new customer. In the overall sales target, repeat customer sales do figure as a major portion. Now let us look at the Customer Relationship Management angle.

Customers are won over not by the product and price alone but by the service and happy experience too.

Any customer who has been happy with the service received is likely to be loyal to the Company and most probably he will be ready to compromise or over look certain defects over superior quality of service. This is not all. When you have one happy customer, you can be sure that in good time he will refer many more customers from his social friends circle as well as family too. This can be a double edged sword. In case a customer is not happy with his experience or the product, he can spread talk ill about the Company as well as the product to his friends and family too.

When you create an E Commerce platform and choose promote your products and services, paying attention to Customer Relationship Management becomes that much more important. Using E Commerce as your sales engine, you are going to focus on wider markets and volume of prospects and customers too. For one thing, with increase in volume of sales, you will need to create the necessary backend process and E enabled System infrastructure to cater to After Sales Service as well as Customer Relationship Management. The internet has changed the consumer behaviour. Customers today expect superior service and immediately. The delivery and service expectations have gone up. Servicing a larger customer base in a short span of time calls for robust CRM system and process backup. It is important to remember that the internet customers have the power of instant communication across the world wide web. What does this mean to your business? It means that you cannot afford to have any lacunae in your product, service or CRM processes. You have got to walk the talk.The customer can influence the entire market with his perceptions and experience.

Integrating CRM with your promotional strategy would go well hand in hand. Along with boosting sales, the marketing managers would need to focus on building brand loyalty and using promotional activities to engage with the Customers as well as delivery enhanced value in the relationship. Every Marketing Manager needs to ask this question - If his Business is equipped and ready for E commerce platform.

E Business Transitions

Migrating to E Business has become inevitable. All

business Organisations have recognised this fact. It has been understood that E Commerce is going to be the sales engine for the future. Understanding and accepting the need to evolve a E Business strategy brings with it more challenges.

The first and foremost challenge that the Organisations face is the question of getting their priorities in order with reference to finances. Capital and funds flow happens to be the backbone and the need for the current ongoing businesses.

At the same time huge funds have to be committed on an ongoing basis to take the Organisation through the E Business strategy which is the need for the future. Managements find it easier to chart out an investment plan for managing the E Transition in phased manner. The commitment and involvement of the top management is very crucial for the E Business implementation. The implementation strategy has got to be top driven.

The second challenge for E Business implementation and transition comes from the commitment of the Senior and Middle Management in the Organisation. E Business transition has to be owned by the functional and administrative managers and calls for continuous involvement during deployment. However in most cases Managers are faced with the day to day business realities of having to chase the targets and committing time and effort for transition programs. The question is, do they have the necessary energy and commitment to own the implementation program?. E implementation programs are such that they have to be owned and implemented by the functional owners and cannot be done independently by a third party. Third party specialists would of course be engaged in the project as consultants but the last mile execution involves the actual operations staff on the ground and hence the functional managers become the owners.

Organisational challenges can be many. However the E implementation strategy has got to take all the factors into account and work around the best strategy that can be implemented. As long as the top management is committed and overseas the entire project, it can be implemented successfully. Take the case of Hewlett Packard. HP management bought Compaq and decided to merge both the companies and create synergy. There were commonalities of course in terms of products etc. However the manufacturing and the supply chain processes followed by both the Companies were totally different. HP chose to integrate both Blue {HP} and Red {Compaq} product lines together and chose to implement SAP across the platform. Blue line had products that were bought out as well as built to stock models of printers and consumables. Red line manufactured computers largely for SOHO segment on build to order basis. Both the product lines had different set of markets as well as supply chain processes. It was important for HP to merge both the supply chains and integrate the warehouses, bring visibility of inventory down to the last mile. At the same time the Company had planned to provide Web visibility of the Order and Delivery confirmations to its Customers.

Implementation was carried out in phased manner in most countries. HP did not opt to enable all modules of SAP R|3. Instead they chose to build interface with the third party service provider's WMS systems for the inventory and warehouse operations. Receipt of goods at a warehouse automatically triggered a message to SAP which enabled the system to drop the orders against the inventory received. Further despatch and delivery tracking was done using the local WMS system. Final Proof of Despatch was uploaded into the HP Website that provided visibility to the end customer. Detailed implementation at country level and across all warehouses in the country called for huge investments into Hardware as well as Software and more importantly in terms of time and cost of the Project teams. With a well organised project workflow that involved senior management involvement at a global level as well as at regional and country level as sponsors, ensured sustained focus, support and resources to the project that spanned over sixteen months in most cases. The commitment to implement and operate through the system drilled down from the top management and superior project planning and implementation skills paved way for success. The end results of the project was that HP gained a lot in terms of leaner resources, faster and flexible processes, visibility of inventory and orders, reduction of lead times for procurement as well as for manufacturing and delivery and lesser cost of production and significant reduction in logistics costs accrued out of higher volumes. Today the teams at HP have forgotten all about the days when they did not have SAP and were managing two supply chains separately. HP has been able to ride the E Commerce wave and ride ahead in the market.

Adapting E Business Model - It is Time to make that Paradigm Shift

Business Managers now days are going back to the business schools to un-learn some of the lessons they had learnt during their class time days and build their ability to make paradigm shift in thinking.

In today's environment where technology and global business scenarios are changing, business rules are being re written. There is no business that has not been affected due to technology. We are slowly beginning to see a change and transition from production and product oriented businesses to high tech, information and service oriented Business Organisations. The expectations of the Organisations from its Managers and Management are changing, keeping in line with the need to adapt to the external environment.

Organisations have got to build the capability to assimilate the new trends, adapt itself, its products and business to be able to survive the new wave. This is creating new demands on the managers wherein they need to bring different skill sets, thought process and leadership in steering the Organisation through the changes and achieve a safe launch.

In the future times, change is going to be constant. The speed of adaptation and change will determine the success of Organisations. The managers have got to be futuristic and be able to understand the technology trends and come up with new E business Modules and Organisations. Continual investment into E technology, focus on providing new service deliveries to the Customers in the face of competition and leveraging technology to stand apart from the crowd is going to be the expectation from the Business Managers.

Doing business on E platform provides a different dimension to the business. The Managers hereto could have participated in planning strategies and not driving the implementation which could be left to the middle management and outsourced partners.

The time taken to implement, obtain results and analyze the results have been quite long. But the scenario in E Trade being different, the results and response on the internet is immediate and instantaneous. Managers have got to focus not only on creating the E Marketing strategy but in implementing it effectively and building the right E Business model to support the E trade initiative. When the business survival today depends upon increasing market share, bringing down the costs, building relationship with customers to enhance service value and build loyalty, the only way that these can be realised is by adapting E Business Design. Building an effective business model calls for integration of technologies, continual up gradation and committed investments in IT architecture.

The new E Business designs call for change in the Management's perspectives towards it entire business. Managements have begun to realise the need to invest into IT infrastructure and move away from investing into manufacturing and production capacities. They have also begun to realise the need to be closer to the customer, understand the changing consumer trends and use this understanding to plan product and service deliveries. Further, the planning horizon is becoming shorter as the need to keep changing the benchmarks, changing the investment priorities and the need to charter the ship through new waters is the call of the day. Understanding E Technology, its capabilities, its future trends has become the urgent need of all those sitting in the Board rooms. It is not about money any more but it is all about E Technology.

Increase Knowledge Base with E Business Model

E business model implementation brings with it several key results and benefits. First and foremost a successful implementation should meet with the Organisational goals that were set during the implementation phase. **Increased customer awareness, capability to handle huge volume of customer orders, build customer relationship etc are some of the well known benefits that accrue out of the successful implementation program**.

The IT partners or the Web Developers who undertake to build, maintain and operate your website provide you with a huge set of reports and data on various metrics. As a Marketing Manager if you are interested in converting your website into a powerful sales engine, then you have got to be keyed into the E business program and build knowledge from it. The website gives you the real and close up picture of your market and customers. Unlike the traditional channels where your customers are at a distance and remote, you are able to see your customer behaviour up close and almost instantaneously. Your customers could range from an individual, an Organisation, Government, Defence or a trader, whole seller, retailer or a mix of all.

The lifecycle of products and services is very short. So also is the buyer's loyalty and buying behaviour. In an every changing and complex scenario, if you have to make strategic decisions about your products, markets and pricing etc, it helps to make decisions based on facts and figures rather than based on past records, performance and understanding of the field sales personnel.

Secondly **building knowledge about your Customer can give you inputs to the changing trends in the market too**. Every day competition gets busy trying to promote sales using different types of sales promotions. Instead of spending money on trying to research and understand customer reactions through surveys, you can use the e reports to gain insights. You can also set up online surveys easily to obtain first hand impression from customers from across the segments.

Trying to build and maintain relationship with your Customer is very important part of your activity. Today's customers are very demanding and are well informed. To hold on to a relationship with your existing customer, you have got to keep providing value to your customer. The E Market platform helps you achieve this very easily and effectively. You are able to identify the segments that your customers belong to, understand their expectations and behaviours very clearly. Understanding your customer expectations makes it easier for you to create a customized value proposition for your each individual customer and thereby enhance the experience that the customer has with you.

Apart from building knowledge on Customer and their needs, you can also gain effective insights that help you tweak your supply chain operations too. Different customers have different strategies and methods of buying. A defense organisation or a Manufacturing organisation might follow E Bid model to buy products while traders and retailers might like to place online orders on weekly basis or buy more depending upon the discount slab offered. Another major customer might want to opt for JIT supplies and expect to send JIT orders in electronic form. Understanding Customer expectations and delivery requirements can give you insight into maintaining leaner inventories, lesser distribution points and effective delivery methods.

On the whole, the more time you spend analyzing and building knowledge using the E reports and data generated, the beneficial it would be for your operations. A smart marketing manager who is in tune with his E market is able to smell the changes in the trends in the market be it with competition or technology as well as with customer expectations. This gives him an edge to be ahead of others in providing the product and services to the customer and exceed customer expectations as well as drive the E strategy as the engine for sales growth.

E Learning Curve

If you scan the developments in the business world that

have taken place in the last fifty years or so, you will find that business Organisations have had to reinvent themselves and write new rules of games. Everything about the business is changing rapidly. Introduction of IT has brought in, undreamt of changes in markets, products, and Organisational structures as well as the approach to business and profits too. Riding on the E Commerce engine seems to be the trajectory for the growth plans that most Organisations are taking on. When we talk about E Commerce and E Marketing, generally the concept that comes to one's mind is the online shopping that we generally engage in. Buying airline tickets, paying utility bills and buying books and CDs etc. If a business manager or a student limits himself to understanding about how On line selling works is not enough.

No doubt E Commerce relates to building website with content using search criteria, driving traffic and promoting your products and services. A larger perspective of how the Organisations and businesses work, the networking with multiple applications and integration that makes things work at the background is

necessary.

In the beginning, the computer applications when introduced were doing only computing functions. Using computers entailed task oriented operations where Garbage In led to Garbage Out. Data entry and computerization of the manual tasks and documents were the outputs provided by the Computers. Slowly we began to see function specific software development. This lead to production being managed by Management Resource Planning softwares and accounting was being computerized using accounting software and so on. All other functions too were computerized using specific functional and stand alone systems. The next stage of development brought with it the cross functional Enterprise Resource Planning Softwares. The developments in the hardware, networking and connectivity helped the evolution of the ERP soft wares.

The important and revolutionary changes that ERP brought with it changed the fundamental approach of the Organisations to the way in which they functioned. ERPs could manage cross functional activities. Soon the systems could be programmed to manage the process which meant the organisations shifted their operations from people to processes. Today using ERP systems to manage operations and all functions has become the basic necessity.

We have also seen emergence of specialized ERP applications too that manage individual functions and can be deployed at global levels. Apart from SAP, Oracle etc Organisations use specific CRM applications like Siebel, HR |Operations Management systems like Ariba as well as Supply chain Management solutions like Red Prairery etc. There are very many soft ware applications that are deployed to integrate the various ERP applications deployed in the Organisation. Besides Organisations use Applications for building business intelligence, Knowledge management and MIS etc.

In the current scenario where the Organisations are operating at multi locations across various markets and geographies and are managing the entire operations using multiple platforms, opening up its business on E Commerce mode brings with it, newer challenges. Amidst the changing environment where newer technologies and new trends keep affecting the markets and consumer behaviour, the

Organisations have got to E enable all of their operations and businesses. It is not enough to just set up a website. The entire operations from procurement, manufacturing, warehousing to order management, financial transactions and third party logistics support would need to be e enabled and integrated to ensure end to end transactions and efficiency of operations. It is quite true that in highly competitive markets, the IT systems and its operational service capabilities become the service differentiators between the leader and rest.

Growing the business into E platform mode is inevitable. Businesses have got to re-orient their marketing strategies and other related plans to use E Marketing and E Trade as the engines for growth in the future.Besides understanding the E realities, being focused on the E Customer and chartering the course for the future is imperative for students, Managers and all professionals to get on to the E learning curve.

Marketing Manager should know about E Procurement Systems

The word customer immediately rings a bell in the

minds of a Marketing Man. Unlike in the earlier times when the Marketing or a Sales executive spent time on the field, visiting and spending time with his customers to understand customer behaviour, today most marketing executives spend time in gathering, analysing the data about customers, in planning and finally meeting the customer with a definitive agenda. The preparation as well as the output expected from customer visits have changed. With the arrival of E Markets, the scenario and the profile of the customer has once again changed.

Marketing managers have now got to keep up to date not only with E marketing strategies but it is also imperative that they get to know a lot more in detail about E procurement.

Be it an individual or an organisation, procurement processes are changing. Internet is enabling them to change their buying processes. Getting to know all of the E procurement practices and the operational processes is very important from a sales and marketing manager's perspective.

While an individual could be looking at your company website or a trading site like E Bay for a best buy option, organisations tend to follow different methods of e procurement. Dell calls for on E bidding for buying services, selecting supply chain partners to manage international, multi modal transportation, Customs Clearance, Warehousing, Documentation, Packaging and Domestic Distribution services. E Bidding allows preferred or invited bidders who have been pre qualified to bid. The online bidding process is spread over several rounds which allows for the bidder to reconsider his bid with the limited feedback provided by the bidder and clarifications provided to the queries. The process is water tight, instantaneous and transparent. The entire bidding process is managed through and using a third party service provider who specialises in E Bidding. Even the DELL teams other than the bid owners do not get to see the details of the bid or influence any outcome or decision. Normally such bids cover huge volumes and high value in terms of sales and services and cover supplies over a period of one or more number of years.

To be able to participate in such E Bids, calls for complete understanding of the bidding process, familiarity with operating the systems as well as complete background homework on the bid proposal and pricing from your end is imperative. As the online bid does not give you any time or chance to go back to your management to seek approvals for price reconsideration etc, you have got to have your decisions with you while going in for E Bidding. This means you will need to have done your pricing homework thoroughly, discussed it thread bear with the management and come to the final pricing. If you are the bidder, you carry the authority to execute the bid and your decisions will be binding on the Company and management. Therefore you need to have clarity of thought, authority and understanding of all the data and facts that enable you to take the decision on your offer. Prior preparation is a Must and Should while going in for online E Bids. It is also important to have the sales team that can support you with you during the E Bid. The decision makers, the costing support as well as operational support teams would need to be at hand to help you take decisions.

GE has implemented an E Procurement system globally that has been proved to be highly effective. GE selects and approves vendors who are enlisted and added on to the E procurement system. Once approved, the vendors get to see the requirements or purchase enquiries floated by GE. Whichever vendor is able to offer best price, best terms and best delivery schedule gets accepted. From amongst the approved vendors, GE has the choice to accept the best offer. The P.order is electronically confirmed and placed on the chosen vendor. The rest of the process of receiving delivery and payment as per pre agreed terms happens automatically through the system.

Getting to know the details of the Customer's E buying process helps you to position yourself suitably to be able to get selected and supply your products and services or in other words, to conclude a sale successfully.

Online Marketing and the Hotel Industry

The Internet/Ecommerce and the Hotel Industry

The rapid spread in the usage of the internet and the increase in access to ecommerce and online bookings has definitely been a boon to the hospitality industry.

The increasing incidence of guests booking their hotel rooms online has not only improved the booking rate of hotels but has also let them pass on hefty discounts to the customers which would otherwise had to be shared with the travel agents and other intermediaries.

In other words, the advent of online booking has been a win-win situation for the hotels and the customers. Next, with so many guests from around the world flocking to the internet to book their rooms and plan their itineraries, hotels are turning to online marketing of their products. This has the effect of reaching out to a wider guest base as the hotels need not constrain their marketing efforts to nearby places and geography is no longer a limiting factor for hotels. The death of distance happened with globalization where the service providers and the customers were brought together by the internet irrespective of where they are and where they wanted to transact business. Similarly, online marketing by hotels has the benefit of the hotels reaching out to customers all over the world and in turn, the tourists and business travelers from anywhere can book their hotel rooms everywhere without any restraint.

Online Marketing by Hotels and its Advantages

Online marketing by hotels has the added advantage of improving the brand image of the hotel by ensuring that customer reviews of the hotels and the glitzy marketing of the hotels have the intended effect of enhancing the reputation of the hotels.

As most of us go by word of mouth recommendations that influence our consumer behavior, favorable customer reviews of hotels on sites like Make my Trip, Travel Advisor, and other content aggregators has the effect of more customers booking rooms in the hotels that attract positive reviews from satisfied customers. Conversely, those hotels that are ranked below and have disgruntled customers writing bad reviews find themselves out of favor with new customers. This "electronic word of mouth" that happens because of travel websites and websites devoted to customers around the world who might be planning their trips to various destinations has greatly contributed to loyal customers and returning customers for the hotels that actualize customer delight and customer satisfaction. Not only that, as marketing theory states that returning customers are very valuable because the marketing effort can then focus on new customers and the returning customers lead to cost efficiencies is a strong point in favor of hotels undertaking extensive online marketing.

Doing away with Intermediaries

As discussed briefly earlier in the article, the hospitality industry is now moving towards a paradigm and a business model where the service providers and the customers interact directly leading to the removal of the intermediary layer. The airline industry was the first to phase out the intermediaries with airlines first reaching out to flyers online and the travel agents facilitating the process. This gradually phased out the travel agent intermediary layer with most bookings now being done online. The hotels are following suit, which means that the costs entailed because of the intermediaries can now be saved leading to value addition to the customers who can avail of the discounts. Indeed, many leading hotels now accept bookings directly on their websites.

Concluding Remarks: The World is Not Enough

As the internet is supposed to add value to all stakeholders in the value chain, the experience of the hospitality industry is a case in point about how the online transactions can result in a win-win situation for all. Further, the concomitant processes of globalization and the increased use of the internet and social media have ensured greater efficiencies in the processes and induced synergies between different players in the value chain. Finally, the world is not enough in this paradigm as the potential opportunities for expansion of the hotels' customer base and the customer experience are unlimited.